The Couples' Toolkit for Coping with ADHD As a Team:

A Holistic Guide to Maintaining Focus, Impulse Control and Thriving with an ADHD Spouse

BY

Anita Mac-Edwards

Copyright © 2023 Anita Mac-Edwards

All rights reserved. Unauthorized reproduction, storage in a retrieval system, or transmission in any form or by any means electronic, mechanical, photocopying, recording, scanning, or otherwise is strictly prohibited without the prior written permission of the publisher, as allowed under Section 107 or 108 of the 1976 United States Copyright Act.

TABLE OF CONTENTS

INTRODUCTION

When I first met my husband Jack, I figured loving a spontaneous free spirit balanced out my tendency to meticulously plan everything. Little did I know that his distractible and impulsive nature, which once intrigued me, would fuel chaos once the pressures of marriage, career, parenthood and more layered up in real life. Behind his playfulness lived undiagnosed ADHD wiring that explained the behaviors leaving me confused and exhausted so often. I just didn't have the neuroscience insight back then.

After years of turmoil and fights neither of us could fully explain, we discovered his unique neurology through getting properly evaluated as an adult. Suddenly the rollercoaster made more sense! His struggles concentrating weren't about personality flaws or indifference toward our family but rather a legitimate disorder impacting key executive functioning and emotional regulation from a young age without conscious choice. Things like forgetting important talks, losing track of time on projects close to deadlines, getting distracted mid-chore repeatedly and especially emotional sensitivity volatility had neurological roots - not relationship ruining motivations after all!

Once equipped with this paradigm shifting education around ADHD, we gained compassionate clarity along with science-backed solutions for nagging issues threatening what was once a beautifully bonded marriage. External structure, medication options, emotional coaching tools and communicating through an insider lens changed everything. We turned knowledge into empowerment.

That's my driving passion helping other neurodivergent couples thrive too - transforming turmoil into tools planting seeds of support, resilience and joy once more. There is light and love awaiting on the other side of breathless chaos if you lean into wisdom! Equipped understanding transforms not only relationships from the brink of collapse but also each partner's self-confidence dismantled over the years by unidentified struggles. Healing happens.

The key rests first in comprehension - grasping what makes the ADHD brain uniquely wired so tendencies often deemed flaky, rude or irresponsible get reframed as opportunities for creative collaboration. Then compassion unfolds more freely once perceived personal attacks against character dissolve revealing symptoms beyond one's control.

Next, practical solutions bringing balance through boundary setting, external structure around known distraction triggers, proper treatment plans aligning to subtype needs and most of all - focusing first on friendship, not just dysfunction junction - fertilizes healthy relationships growing despite myopically seeing only another's weaknesses initially. Once education awakens empathy, motivation for positive change will organically emerge from both partners.

If one half of your duo currently remains undiagnosed or misunderstood, I see you exhausted from years subconsciously carrying an overwhelming household, financial and emotional burden solo without context around why. And chances are high accompanied resentment brews beneath surface band-aids because support feels one-directional. Partners don't intend hurting one another yet patterns predictably play out damaging connection's cords fraying till potential sever.

My friend, whether ADHD roams your reality or anxious anguish inhabits your home, there is hope ahead. Untangling neurobiology provides pathways forward few treads without a guide. But by this book's journey end, my goal is equipping your relationship with resilient tools and wisdom to not only survive but truly thrive amidst our complicated yet incredible differences. If I found harmony, I believe you can too! **Your next chapter awaits...**

CHAPTER ONE

Revealing the ADHD Brain: A Spouse's

Perspective

Honey, can you remember that time I accidentally dyed my hair purple instead of brown? It was supposed to be a quick "pick-me-up" after a long week, and well, let's just say the instructions were a bit too "minimalist" for my ADHD husband's interpretation.

Okay, before you start picturing me living a life of chaos and hair dye disasters, let me assure you, it's not all bad. In fact, being married to someone with ADHD has been one of the most enriching experiences of my life. It's opened my eyes to a whole new world of perspectives, forced me to become incredibly flexible, and most importantly, shown me the incredible strength and resilience of the human spirit (both mine and his!).

But let's be honest, there have definitely been some bumps along the way. Like hitting the brakes on the highway because a squirrel decided to cross the road in front of us, or finding his prized collection of vintage comic books inexplicably living in the freezer (don't ask!).

So, if you're feeling a little lost, frustrated, or maybe even downright confused in your relationship with an ADHD partner, well, you're not alone. But before we dive into the "how-tos" and practical tips, I want to take a step back and explore the amazing, and yes, sometimes challenging, world inside their heads.

Imagine your brain as a finely tuned orchestra, with different sections working together to create a beautiful symphony of thoughts, emotions, and actions. Now, imagine this orchestra conductor is a bit...enthusiastic. He has a million ideas a minute, wants to play every instrument at once, and sometimes gets a little carried away with the tempo.

That's kind of what it's like for someone with ADHD. Their brains are wired differently, with unique strengths and weaknesses that can sometimes make daily life a little, well, unpredictable.

Remember that time you had that extra strong cup of coffee and felt your heart racing, your thoughts jumping, and your body buzzing with energy? That's a tiny glimpse into the world of someone with ADHD. Their nervous system is constantly on high alert, processing information at a rapid pace. This can lead to sensory overload, making them easily overwhelmed by noise, lights, or crowded environments.

It can also explain why losing track of time seems like a national sport for them. They're constantly bombarded with internal and external stimuli, making it difficult to focus on one thing for an extended period. Think of it like trying to read a book with a rock concert playing in the background – not exactly conducive to focusing, right?

Now, here's the interesting part: despite the noise and chaos, the ADHD brain actually **craves** stimulation. It's like a car that needs constant fuel to keep running. This explains why they might seem restless, fidgety, or always looking for the next exciting thing. Think of it as their way of trying to regulate their own internal chaos.

Okay, so let's talk superpowers. The heightened sense of excitement, impulsivity, and constant need for stimulation that can sometimes be frustrating can also be incredible assets. These same traits often translate into boundless creativity, a knack for problem-solving outside the box, and an infectious enthusiasm that can light up a room.

My husband, for example, can come up with the most creative solutions to everyday problems, his passion for his hobbies is contagious, and his zest for life is simply inspiring.

But, like any double-edged sword, these superpowers come with their own set of challenges. Impulsivity can lead to poor decision-making, hyperactivity can make it difficult to sit still in meetings, and the constant need for stimulation can sometimes feel like a relentless energy drain on their partners.

Now, this wouldn't be a proper peek inside the ADHD brain without mentioning the science behind it all. Research suggests that one of the key players is dopamine, a neurotransmitter that plays a crucial role in motivation, focus, and reward. In the ADHD brain, dopamine levels may be lower or work differently compared to someone without ADHD.

This can explain why focusing on tasks feels like a constant uphill battle, completing projects can be incredibly challenging, and staying organized seems like an impossible feat. It's not that they don't want to focus, it's just that their brains are wired to make it more difficult.

But the dopamine story doesn't end there. Studies also show differences in blood flow and neuronal activity in the brains of people with ADHD. Areas responsible for attention, planning, and impulse control may show less activity compared to individuals without ADHD. This explains why focusing on long-term goals, planning future events, and resisting immediate temptations can be more challenging for them.

The Unique Wiring Inside the ADHD Mind

Let's be honest, sometimes it feels like your partner and you are operating on entirely different operating systems. You focus like a laser on one task at a time, while they seem to switch gears faster than a racecar driver. This isn't because they're not trying to focus, but because their brains are wired differently.

Imagine the brain as a bustling city with information constantly zipping around like cars on highways. In a neurotypical brain (meaning a brain without ADHD), these highways are well-maintained, with designated lanes for different types of information. Traffic flows smoothly, and the city functions efficiently.

Now, picture your partner's brain as a city during rush hour on a holiday weekend. Every road is packed, cars are honking, and there's a constant buzz of activity. It's **loud, stimulating, and chaotic**. But here's the thing: it doesn't mean there's anything wrong with the city! It just operates differently.

How ADHD Affects the Senses and Nervous System?

People with ADHD often experience the world in a more intense way. Imagine turning up the volume on all your senses at once. Colors might seem a bit brighter, sounds might be sharper, and even textures might feel more pronounced. This sensory overload can be overwhelming at times, making it difficult to filter out distractions and focus on one thing.

Furthermore, the ADHD brain has a hypersensitive fight-or-flight response. Remember that scene in your favorite action movie where the hero jumps at the slightest noise? That's kind of what's happening in your partner's brain all the time. They're constantly on high alert, which can lead to restlessness, impulsivity, and difficulty staying still.

Why the ADHD Brain Craves Stimulation?

Now, here's where things get interesting. People with ADHD often have difficulties with something called dopamine regulation. Dopamine is a neurotransmitter that plays a crucial role in motivation, reward, and focus. For a neurotypical brain, completing a task or meeting a goal naturally releases dopamine, creating a sense of accomplishment and driving further action.

However, in an ADHD brain, the dopamine system isn't quite as efficient. It's like having a leaky faucet — dopamine gets released too quickly, or not enough is produced in the first place. **This leads to a constant craving for stimulation** as the brain seeks out activities that can trigger a dopamine release, even if they seem unproductive or impulsive from the outside.

Think of it like this: Imagine your partner's brain is like a car that needs a constant flow of fuel to stay running smoothly. For you, a leisurely drive to the park might be enough to recharge your batteries. But your partner? They might need an adrenaline-pumping adventure park experience to get the same dopamine boost.

The Superpowers and Challenges of the ADHD Brain

Okay, so we've established that an ADHD brain is different — not "broken," just different. And guess what? This difference comes with a **unique set of strengths**. People with ADHD are often:

- ✓ **Highly creative and innovative:** Their constant stream of ideas and out-of-the-box thinking can be a major asset in any field.
- ✓ **Full of boundless energy:** Their enthusiasm and zest for life can be infectious, bringing a spark of excitement to any situation.
- ✓ **Hyper-focused when they're engaged:** When they find something they're truly passionate about, they can devote laser-like focus and dedication.
- ✓ **Empathetic and compassionate:** Their heightened awareness of their own emotions often translates into a deep understanding of others' feelings.

Of course, these strengths can also come with their own set of challenges. The same energy that fuels their creativity can lead to impulsiveness. Their hyper-focus can sometimes morph into hyper-fixation, neglecting other important tasks. And their heightened emotions can lead ### to emotional dysregulation, making it difficult to manage frustration or disappointment.

So, what does all this mean for you, the amazing partner navigating this exciting (and sometimes challenging) journey with your ADHD partner? It means that *understanding and appreciating their unique wiring is the key to building a harmonious and fulfilling relationship*. Here are some tips to help you unlock the magic within your partnership:

1. **Embrace the neurodiversity:** Instead of trying to "fix" your partner or force them to conform to your way of doing things, celebrate their unique perspective and strengths. Remember, their brain operates differently, not defectively.

2. **Communication is key:** Open and honest communication is essential in any relationship, but it's especially crucial when dealing with ADHD. Talk

to your partner about their needs, frustrations, and triggers, and be open to listening to theirs.

3. **Find a common language:** Don't just talk at each other, talk with each other. Learn to understand each other's communication styles. Your partner might prefer visual aids or shorter, more direct conversations, while you might need more elaboration and reassurance.

4. **Teamwork makes the dream work:** Approach challenges as a team, not adversaries. Brainstorm solutions together, be patient with setbacks, and celebrate each other's successes, big or small.

5. **Celebrate the little things:** Don't get bogged down by the daily grind. Take time to appreciate the little quirks and spontaneous adventures that make your partner unique. Remember, their impulsiveness can sometimes lead to unexpected fun and excitement!

6. **Embrace flexibility:** Life with ADHD is rarely predictable. Be prepared to adjust your plans and

expectations when needed. Remember, flexibility is key to navigating the ups and downs of any relationship, not just one with ADHD.

7. **Create a supportive environment:** Help your partner create a system that works for them. This might involve setting up routines, utilizing visual reminders, or creating designated workspaces that minimize distractions.

8. **Be patient and understanding:** Change takes time and effort. Don't get discouraged if progress feels slow. Be patient with your partner and yourself, and celebrate even the smallest steps forward.

9. **Seek professional help if needed:** If you're struggling to cope or navigate the challenges of ADHD within your relationship, don't hesitate to seek professional help. Therapists who specialize in ADHD can provide valuable guidance and support for both individuals and couples.

10. Remember, you're not alone: There are countless resources available for partners of individuals with ADHD. Online communities, support groups, and even couples therapy specifically designed for neurodiverse relationships can offer valuable information, connection, and guidance.

Living with an ADHD partner can be a whirlwind of emotions, a rollercoaster ride of excitement, frustration, and everything in between. But remember, understanding, acceptance, and a healthy dose of humor can go a long way in building a strong and fulfilling relationship.

Your partner's ADHD is just one aspect of who they are. It doesn't define them, and it certainly doesn't define your relationship. Embrace their unique qualities, celebrate their strengths, and together, create a love story filled with adventure, understanding, and unwavering support. Because at the end of the day, love truly knows no bounds, ADHD or not.

ACTIVITY PLAN FOR CHAPTER 1

Activity 1: Understanding the Unique Wiring
Task:

- Read a book or watch a documentary together about the ADHD brain.

- Discuss key takeaways and how they relate to your spouse's experiences.

Benefits:

- Increases understanding and empathy.

- Creates a shared language to discuss ADHD-related challenges.

Real-Life Example:

Choose a book such as "Driven to Distraction" by Edward Hallowell and John Ratey or watch a documentary like "ADD & Loving It?!" together. Take notes or highlight sections that resonate with your spouse's experiences. Afterward, have a relaxed conversation over a cup of tea, discussing how the insights from the material can be applied to daily life. This not only educates but also strengthens your connection through shared learning.

Activity 2: Sensory Exploration Activities

Task:

- Create a sensory toolkit with items like stress balls, fidget toys, or scented candles.
- Practice mindful breathing exercises together to regulate the nervous system.

Benefits:

- Provides tools for self-regulation.
- Reduces stress and anxiety.

Real-Life Example:

Gather items that cater to different sensory needs, such as a textured stress ball, a smooth worry stone, or a scented candle. Label each item with its intended purpose (e.g., "Stress Relief" or "Focus Aid"). Encourage your spouse to use these tools when feeling overwhelmed or scattered. Additionally, practice deep breathing exercises together. Sit in a comfortable space, close your eyes, and take slow, deep breaths together. This activity can be a calming ritual before bed or during moments of tension.

Activity 3: Stimulation Strategies

Task:

- Create a "Brain Boost" board with activities that stimulate the mind.
- Schedule regular breaks for movement and sensory input.

Benefits:

- Channels excess energy into productive activities.
- Improves focus and productivity.

Real-Life Example:

Together, brainstorm and create a "Brain Boost" board filled with activities that engage the mind and body. This could include puzzles, brain teasers, art projects, or physical activities like yoga or dancing. Hang the board in a visible place and encourage your spouse to choose an activity when they need a mental break or a burst of energy. Additionally, schedule "movement breaks" throughout the day. Set a timer for a quick walk, jumping jacks, or stretching exercises to break up periods of sitting.

Activity 4: Embracing Superpowers and Addressing Challenges

Task:

- Create a "Strengths Collage" highlighting your spouse's unique talents and qualities.
- Brainstorm practical solutions together for common ADHD challenges.

Benefits:

- Boosts self-esteem and confidence.
- Encourages proactive problem-solving.

Real-Life Example:

Gather magazines, photos, and quotes that represent your spouse's strengths and positive qualities. Create a collage together, adding personal touches and affirmations. Display this collage in a prominent place as a daily reminder of their capabilities. Next, tackle common ADHD challenges as a team. Sit down with a notepad and list out specific challenges your spouse faces, such as forgetfulness or time management. Brainstorm together practical solutions or systems that could help, such as setting reminders on phones or using visual schedules.

Activity 5: Nutrition and Gut Health

Task:

- Explore ADHD-friendly nutrition by trying new recipes together.
- Keep a food journal to track how different foods impact mood and focus.

Benefits:

- Supports brain function and overall well-being.
- Increases awareness of the mind-body connection.

Real-Life Example:

Research ADHD-friendly foods and recipes, such as those rich in omega-3 fatty acids (found in fish like salmon), whole grains, and fresh fruits and vegetables. Pick a new recipe to try together each week and make it a fun cooking experiment. Keep a food journal where your spouse can note how they feel after eating certain foods. This can help identify patterns of how food impacts their energy levels, focus, and mood.

Congratulations on completing the action plan for Chapter 1! By engaging in these activities, you are not only supporting your ADHD spouse but also fostering a deeper understanding of their unique brain wiring. Remember, each step you take together is a step toward a harmonious and thriving home environment.

CHAPTER TWO

A Day-in-the-Life with ADHD Obstacles

Now, before you start picturing chaotic living spaces and overflowing to-do lists (although, let's be honest, it's not always sunshine and rainbows!), I want to emphasize that everyone's experience is unique. Just like snowflakes, each individual with ADHD has their own quirks, strengths, and challenges.

So, let's take a peek into a typical day in the life of someone with ADHD. Imagine waking up with a mind that's already buzzing with a million thoughts, like a beehive on a sunny day. This isn't necessarily anxiety; it's just the way their brain is wired.

Focusing on getting ready can be like trying to herd cats. One minute they're searching for their keys, the next they're engrossed in a fascinating article about the history of buttons (don't ask!), completely forgetting about the clock ticking away.

Breakfast can be a whirlwind of missed deadlines ("Honey, your ride to work is here!"), unfinished meals ("I'll just grab a granola bar on the way!"), and misplaced essentials ("Where did I put my phone again?!").

The workday might involve periods of intense hyperfocus, where they're completely engrossed in a task, oblivious to everything around them. This can be amazing when it comes to creative brainstorming or problem-solving, but it can also lead to missed deadlines or forgotten meetings if their focus isn't harnessed effectively.

And then there's the constant battle with distractions. Remember that squirrel story from Chapter 1? Now imagine it happening throughout the day – a chirping bird outside the window, a coworker's ringtone, a random thought about that fascinating button article – all vying for their attention.

The evening might bring a sigh of relief, but the internal energy doesn't always cooperate. Winding down can be a struggle, making it difficult to focus on quality time with loved ones. Instead, they might gravitate towards activities that provide immediate stimulation, like video games or scrolling through social media, even if it leads to feelings of guilt or exhaustion later.

Now, here's what you, as a supportive spouse, might not always see: the *tremendous effort* it takes to navigate this internal world. The constant hyperfocus can be incredibly draining, like running a marathon without ever reaching the finish line.

And then there's the constant switching of gears, going from one task to another with lightning speed. While this can seem like an attention deficit, it's actually a result of their brain constantly seeking stimulation and novelty. This constant shifting can be exhausting, not just for them, but also for those around them who struggle to keep up.

Here's a crucial point to remember: **having ADHD doesn't make someone lazy, unorganized, or unintelligent**. It simply means their brain works differently. Imagine trying to read a book with dyslexia; you're not "dumb," the information is just processed differently. It's the same concept with ADHD.

One of the biggest frustrations for partners is the *myth of intentionality* When they forget something, arrive late, or lose their keys, it's not because they don't care or are intentionally trying to be difficult. The reality is, they might genuinely forget, get hyper-focused and lose track of time, or simply misplace things due to challenges with executive function.

Now, let's talk about emotions. People with ADHD often experience emotional dysregulation meaning their emotions can be more intense and fluctuate more rapidly than someone without ADHD. This can manifest as frustration, impatience, or even outbursts in moments of stress or overwhelm.

It's important to understand that these emotional responses are not directed at you, but rather a result of their brain struggling to process and regulate emotions effectively. This can be incredibly challenging for partners, as it can feel like walking on eggshells, unsure of what might trigger an emotional response.

However, remember, this isn't about placing blame or making excuses. It's about understanding and having compassion. Imagine yourself trying to navigate a crowded, noisy market with every sensory input amplified tenfold. That's the experience for someone with ADHD in moments of overwhelm. Now, imagine the person you love standing in that market with you, trying their best to navigate the chaos. Wouldn't you want to offer them support and understanding, rather than judgment?

That's the key to building a strong and supportive relationship with someone who has ADHD. It's about understanding their experience, empathizing with their challenges, and celebrating their unique strengths.

Before we move on, I want to shift the focus from the challenges to the incredible gifts that come with being partnered with someone with ADHD. See, that "always-on" brain also translates into boundless creativity, an infectious enthusiasm for life, and a unique way of looking at the world.

My husband, for instance, can turn everyday chores into hilarious adventures. He approaches problems with an "outside the box" perspective, often surprising me with innovative solutions. His passion for his hobbies is contagious, and his zest for life never fails to inspire me.

So, while there are undoubtedly challenges, it's important to remember that ADHD also comes with a treasure trove of unique strengths that can enrich your life in unexpected ways.

Let's talk about the cornerstone of any healthy relationship: communication. But navigating communication in a relationship with ADHD can feel like trying to cross a river with a leaky boat. It requires patience, understanding, and a willingness to adapt.

Here are some tips that have worked for me:

- ✓ **Focus on "I" statements:** Instead of blaming accusations like "You never!" or "You're so disorganized!", try statements that express how their behavior makes you feel, like "I feel frustrated when things get cluttered, as it makes it hard for me to relax."
- ✓ **Active listening:** Truly listen to their perspective without interrupting. This doesn't mean agreeing with everything they say, but simply acknowledging their feelings and experiences.
- ✓ **Choose your battles:** Don't fight every small issue. Pick your battles and address the most important concerns calmly and constructively.
- ✓ **Focus on solutions, not problems:** Instead of dwelling on what went wrong, work together to find solutions that work for both of you. Brainstorm ideas and be open to compromise.

Remember, communication is a two-way street. While it's important to express your needs and concerns, it's equally important to encourage them to share their feelings and experiences openly and honestly.

A Day-in-the-Life with ADHD Obstacles:

Imagine this: the alarm clock blares, pulling your partner from a night of vivid dreams (where they probably saved the world, negotiated a peace treaty, and invented a flying potato peeler – all before breakfast!). They spring out of bed, ready to tackle the day with the enthusiasm of a puppy encountering a squeaky toy for the first time.

But hold on a minute! Where are those car keys? Weren't they on the counter? Wait, no, there! Nestled comfortably in the freezer next to last week's leftover pizza. Welcome to the "lost and found" reality of many individuals with ADHD. Misplaced objects become a daily obstacle course, testing their patience and sometimes causing a cascade of frustration (and a touch of hilarity, if you can find the humor in it!).

Breakfast might be a quick granola bar eaten on the go, while their mind races with a million to-do list items. The shower might involve singing their favorite power ballad at the top of their lungs (because why not?). And getting dressed might entail a fashion show of mismatched socks and a shirt worn inside out (hey, at least it's comfortable!).

The Exhaustion of Constant Hyperfocus and Switching Gears

Now, picture this: your partner starts working on a project. They're *hyper-focused*, completely absorbed in the task at hand. Time seems to melt away, and they're in a state of pure bliss – until... *ding* goes the phone. Suddenly, the hyperfocus breaks, replaced by the siren song of a new notification. They switch gears, tackling the email with the same level of intensity, only to be interrupted by a sudden urge to tidy up the living room (because, you know, inspiration strikes in the most unexpected moments!).

This *constant switching of gears* can be incredibly draining, both for your partner and for you, the observer. It may seem like they lack focus or commitment, but remember, it's not that they don't want to finish the task; it's their brain's natural tendency to seek novelty and stimulation.

Untangling the Myth from Reality about ADHD

Let's bust some myths, shall we? Here are a few common misconceptions about ADHD that you might encounter:

Myth #1: *People with ADHD are lazy and lack motivation.*

Reality: Not true! While staying focused on certain tasks can be challenging,

individuals with ADHD often have **abundant motivation**, especially when engaged in activities they find interesting or stimulating.

Myth #2: *They can't hold down a job or maintain relationships.*

Reality: Absolutely false! With the right support, individuals with ADHD can be highly successful** in their careers and relationships. It's about understanding their unique needs and creating an environment that allows them to thrive.

<u>Myth #3:</u> *Medication is the only solution.*

Reality: While medication can be a valuable tool for managing ADHD symptoms, it's not always necessary or the only option. Therapy, lifestyle changes, and support systems can also play a crucial role in achieving success.

How Emotional Dysregulation Impacts Relationships

Let's talk about something that can be particularly challenging for both individuals with ADHD and their partners: emotional dysregulation. Remember the hypersensitive fight-or-flight response we discussed before? Well, sometimes, that response can manifest as emotional outbursts, frustration, or difficulty managing stress.

Imagine this: your partner is having a rough day at work. Deadlines are looming, projects are piling up, and their to-do list seems to be multiplying like a gremlin after midnight. This can lead to feelings of overwhelm, frustration, and even anger. They might snap at you for something seemingly insignificant, leaving you feeling hurt and confused.

It's important to remember that these emotional outbursts are not personal attacks. They're a symptom of the underlying struggle with managing their emotions. The key here is to communicate openly and honestly, express your feelings without judgment, and help them develop healthy coping mechanisms for managing their emotions.

ACTION PLAN FOR CHAPTER 2

Activity 1: A Day-in-the-Life Insights
Task:

- Role-play a typical day in the life of someone with ADHD, either yourself or with your spouse.

- Experience firsthand the challenges of distractions, hyperfocus, and shifting tasks.

Benefits:

- Gain empathy and understanding for the daily struggles of ADHD.

- Open up discussions on how to support each other better.

Real-Life Example:

Imagine waking up and trying to get ready for work with a mind buzzing with thoughts about a project. You find it hard to focus on getting dressed because you're already planning the day ahead. Then, during breakfast, the phone pings with notifications, and you get sucked into responding to emails, forgetting about the time. By the time you're ready to leave, you're already feeling frazzled and late.

Activity 2: Hyperfocus Management

Task:

- Create a "Hyperfocus Jar" or timer to help manage periods of intense focus.
- Set specific times for hyperfocus activities and transitions to other tasks.

Benefits:

- Prevents getting "stuck" in tasks for too long.
- Encourages smoother transitions between activities.

Real-Life Example:

Imagine setting a timer for 30 minutes when starting a task. When the timer goes off, it's a signal to take a break or switch to another activity. This helps in managing hyperfocus so that other responsibilities don't get neglected.

Activity 3: Myth Busting Game

Task:

- Create a list of common myths about ADHD.
- Research together to find facts and myths, then play a game to match them.

Benefits:

- Promotes learning and understanding of ADHD facts.
- Provides a lighthearted way to dispel misconceptions.

Real-Life Example:

List myths like "ADHD is just an excuse for laziness" or "People with ADHD can't focus on anything." Then, research together to find the truths behind these statements. During game time, match the myth with the fact, discussing each one as you go.

Activity 4: Emotional Regulation Tools
Task:

- Create an "Emotion Toolbox" with calming techniques and coping strategies.
- Practice using these tools during moments of emotional dysregulation.

Benefits:

- Enhances emotional awareness and regulation.

- Provides practical ways to manage emotional outbursts or shutdowns.

Real-Life Example:

In your toolbox, include deep breathing exercises, mindfulness activities, and a list of calming phrases or affirmations. When emotions run high, take a break together to practice these techniques. For example, sit down, close your eyes, and take deep breaths together for a few minutes.

Congratulations on completing the action plan for Chapter 2! By engaging in these activities, you're taking proactive steps to understand and manage the unique experiences of ADHD. Remember, it's a journey of learning and growth together as partners.

CHAPTER THREE

Embracing Your Differences as Strengths

Okay, warriors of love! Gather 'round and let me spill the tea on what it's like living in a neurodiverse partnership. It's like tango meets tap dancing — sometimes graceful and synchronized, other times a hilariously chaotic blend of steps. But hey, that's the beauty of it, right?

My husband, bless his heart, is the epitome of sunshine and boundless energy. I, on the other hand, am more of a "slow and steady wins the race" kind of gal. This difference in energy levels used to be a major source of frustration. He'd want to go on spontaneous hikes while I craved a quiet evening with a good book. It felt like we were constantly pulling in opposite directions.

But, as they say, love is all about compromise. We started scheduling *"we time"* activities that catered to both our needs. We'd have cozy movie nights at home followed by adventurous weekend trips, finding that sweet spot where both our energy levels could meet.

Communication, however, was a whole other ball game. I'm a straight shooter, while my husband has a way of... well, let's just say his brain sometimes takes the scenic route. It led to a lot of misunderstandings and hurt feelings.

Then, we stumbled upon the magic of **"I" statements.** Instead of accusatory outbursts like "You never!" or "You're always so disorganized!", we learned to express how each other's actions made us feel. "I feel frustrated when things get cluttered because it makes it hard for me to relax," became my go-to phrase. It wasn't about blame games, but about opening a dialogue and understanding each other's perspectives.

Embracing our differences became the key to finding harmony. My husband's infectious enthusiasm taught me to loosen up and embrace spontaneity, while he learned to appreciate my need for calm and organization. We realized our differences weren't weaknesses, but rather unique strengths that complemented each other.

It's not always sunshine and rainbows, but the journey of navigating a neurodiverse partnership has been an enriching adventure. We've learned to navigate our "energetic push and pull," appreciate our differing communication styles, and celebrate our unique strengths. Most importantly, we've learned to laugh at the occasional mishaps and embrace the beautiful tapestry of our love story, one step (or tango, or tap dance) at a time.

Think of it like a ballet. Both partners bring their individual talents, strengths, and even quirks to the stage. One dances with meticulous precision, the other embraces improvisation. While their styles might seem different at first glance, when they learn to move together in harmony, the result can be truly breathtaking.

The key to a thriving neurodiverse partnership is understanding that differences are not deficiencies, they are strengths. Your partner's unique perspective, quirky humor, and boundless energy can bring a vibrant and exciting rhythm to your relationship. Learn to appreciate their "neuro-dance moves" for what they are — ways of navigating the world that might be different from your own, but equally valuable.

For example, my husband might approach tasks with a carefree spontaneity that sometimes makes me want to grab a fire extinguisher (metaphorically, of course!), but his ability to think outside the box often leads to ingenious solutions. His boundless enthusiasm, while sometimes exhausting, is also incredibly infectious, and his zest for life reminds me to embrace the joy in everyday moments.

Talking about the communication waltz. This can be one of the trickiest steps in a neurodiverse partnership. We all have our own communication styles, and when they differ significantly, like in an ADHD relationship, it can feel like trying to tango with a waltz partner – the steps simply don't quite match.

Navigating the Energetic Push and Pull

One of the unique challenges in a neurodiverse partnership is navigating the **energetic push and pull**. You might be a "low-battery" partner, content with cozy evenings in, while your partner thrives on high-octane activities. This can sometimes feel like a tug-of-war, with you yearning for peace and quiet while they crave adrenaline-pumping adventures.

Here are some strategies to find harmony in your energy levels:

a. **Schedule "me time":** Make space for individual activities that cater to each of your energy levels. This could be a quiet afternoon with a book for you, while your partner enjoys an afternoon hike.

b. **Plan "we time":** Find activities that cater to your combined energy levels. Maybe it's a weekend spent exploring a new city, or a relaxing evening playing board games with friends.

c. **Compromise and negotiate:** Don't be afraid to compromise and negotiate your activity choices. You might agree to attend your partner's high-energy event for a shorter time, while they meet you halfway by joining you for a quiet dinner afterwards.

d. **Communicate your needs:** Openly communicate your energy levels and negotiate activities that work for both of you. Respect your individual needs while also making an effort to find ways to enjoy some activities together.

Strategies for Harmonizing with Your Partner

Remember, a successful neurodiverse partnership isn't about trying to mold your partner into someone they're not. It's about finding ways to harmonize your unique styles like blending different musical instruments to create a beautiful symphony.

Here are some helpful strategies:

1. **Establish clear boundaries:** Having clear boundaries is crucial in any relationship, but especially in a neurodiverse partnership. Discuss and communicate your expectations regarding things like time management, organization, and household chores.

2. **Celebrate and encourage effort, not just outcomes:** When your partner makes an effort to manage their ADHD symptoms, acknowledge and celebrate their progress, even if the outcome isn't perfect. This positive reinforcement will encourage them to continue their efforts and foster a sense of accomplishment.

3. **Embrace flexibility:** Be prepared to adjust to unexpected situations and embrace flexibility. Remember, life in a neurodiverse partnership can be an exciting, but sometimes unpredictable, journey.

4. **Seek external support**: Don't hesitate to seek professional help from a therapist or counselor specializing in neurodiverse relationships. They can provide valuable tools and strategies for communication, conflict resolution, and fostering a healthy and fulfilling partnership.

5. **Invest in personal growth:** Continuously learn and grow as individuals. Read books, attend workshops, and engage in activities that allow you to better understand ADHD and navigate the dynamics of a neurodiverse relationship.

6. **Nurture your sense of humor:** Remember, laughter is the best medicine! Don't be afraid to laugh at the unexpected quirks and mishaps that might arise from your partner's "unique wiring." A shared sense of humor can go a long way in diffusing tension, maintaining perspective, and keeping the relationship lighthearted.

More Than Just "Surviving," It's Thriving

Building a thriving neurodiverse partnership is an ongoing process that requires dedication, understanding, and a willingness to adapt. There will be moments of frustration, yes, but there will also be moments of pure joy, laughter, and a sense of connection that transcends differences.

It's not just about "surviving;" it's about thriving in the vibrant tapestry of your unique love story. Remember, you're not alone in this journey. There are countless resources available to help you on your way, including online communities, support groups, and professional guidance.

So, hold your partner's hand, embrace your differences, and pirouette into the exciting dance of your neurodiverse partnership. It might require some fancy footwork and occasional stumbles, but the joy, connection, and unique melody of your love will be truly unforgettable.

Additional Tips:

- ✓ Focus on building a strong foundation of trust and respect. This will allow you to navigate challenges with greater ease and openness.
- ✓ Remember that patience, empathy, and compassion are key. Put yourself in your partner's shoes and try to understand their perspective.
- ✓ Celebrate small wins and progress along the way. This will keep you motivated and focused on the positive aspects of your relationship.
- ✓ Remember, you are a team. Work together to navigate challenges and support each other in reaching your goals.

Building a thriving neurodiverse partnership is a journey, not a destination. It takes time, effort, and a willingness to learn and grow together. But through dedicated communication, collaboration, and a celebration of your unique strengths, you can create a love story that is truly extraordinary.

ACTION PLAN FOR CHAPTER 3

Activity 1: Embracing Differences Workshop
Task:

- Set aside dedicated time for a workshop or discussion on embracing neurodiversity.

- Create a safe space to share strengths, challenges, and ways to support each other.

Benefits:

- Enhances mutual understanding and appreciation.

- Builds a foundation of acceptance and celebration of differences.

Real-Life Example:
Host a workshop at home where each of you prepares a presentation or shares stories about your unique strengths. For instance, if one of you has hyperfocus tendencies, celebrate how it contributes to deep work or creativity. If the other struggles with time management, highlight how their spontaneity brings joy and flexibility to the relationship.

Activity 2: Communication Style Discovery

Task:

- Take an online communication style quiz together.

- Discuss the results and how you can adapt your communication to each other's styles.

Benefits:

- Improves communication and reduces misunderstandings.

- Encourages empathy and flexibility in interactions.

Real-Life Example:

Use a communication style quiz or tool like the Myers-Briggs Type Indicator (MBTI) or the Five Love Languages quiz. Discuss the results openly, focusing on how each of your styles influences your interactions. For instance, if one of you is more visual and prefers written communication, explore ways to incorporate this into daily exchanges.

Activity 3: Navigating Energetic Dynamics

Task:

- Create a "Balance Board" to visually represent your energy levels throughout the day.
- Discuss strategies to support each other during high and low energy periods.

Benefits:

- Promotes awareness and understanding of energy fluctuations.
- Enables proactive support and harmony during different energy phases.

Real-Life Example:

Draw a balance board with a scale of 1 to 10, indicating energy levels. Throughout the day, place a marker on where each of you feels on the scale. Use this visual aid to plan activities or discussions during times of optimal energy. For instance, if one of you is more energetic in the morning, schedule important conversations or activities during this time.

Activity 4: Harmonizing Activities

Task:

- Plan joint activities that cater to both partners' interests and strengths.
- Rotate roles to experience each other's perspectives and challenges.

Benefits:

- Fosters connection and shared experiences.
- Encourages empathy and appreciation for each other's strengths.

Real-Life Example:

If one of you loves outdoor activities while the other prefers quiet evenings at home, find a middle ground. Plan a hike in a scenic area where you can enjoy nature together, followed by a cozy picnic or movie night at home. Rotate roles in planning activities to ensure both partners feel heard and valued.

Congratulations on completing the action plan for Chapter 3! By engaging in these activities, you're taking proactive steps to navigate the unique dynamics of a neurodiverse partnership. Remember, the key is to embrace and celebrate your differences as strengths that complement each other.

CHAPTER FOUR

Connecting Through the Chaos

I Remember a time we were running late for his sister's wedding and his keys were missing in action? We tore the house apart, me on the verge of a meltdown, while he remained strangely calm, finally unearthing them from the crisper drawer of the refrigerator. (Don't ask.) It was moments like these that made me feel like we were living in two different realities, connected by a love that sometimes felt buried under the chaos.

But here's the thing: despite the challenges, our connection is **stronger than ever.** We've learned to navigate the "beautiful chaos" of our relationship, not just survive it, but **thrive** in it. It all started with understanding.

I embarked on a journey to learn about ADHD, not to turn into a medical professional, but to gain a basic understanding of what Alex was experiencing. It wasn't about judging him, but about building empathy and compassion. I discovered the "always-on" nature of his brain, the constant whirlwind of thoughts and stimuli that could sometimes make focusing on a single task, like finding his keys, incredibly difficult.

Armed with this newfound knowledge, we started creating external structure and routine. We adopted the **vision board method**, plastering our living room wall with pictures of our dream vacation in Greece (complete with breathtaking sunsets and endless plates of moussaka, of course!). This visual reminder served as a constant source of motivation, helping Alex stay focused on the bigger picture and making the daily grind a little more meaningful.

We also started **scheduling "we time"** into our calendars, blocking out dedicated time for activities we both enjoyed. Movie nights became a weekly ritual, a chance to unwind and connect without the distractions of everyday life. It wasn't always grand gestures, but these small moments of shared experience built a foundation of connection, a quiet haven amidst the whirlwind.

Celebrating progress, even the small wins, became crucial. When Alex remembered to take his medication on time, we'd do a little victory dance (yes, literally!), acknowledging his efforts and boosting his sense of accomplishment. It might sound silly, but these celebrations fostered a sense of teamwork and encouraged him to keep striving.

Now, let's address the elephant in the room: **intimacy.** Traditional forms of physical connection weren't always smooth sailing, thanks to hi difficulties with focus and maintaining attention. So, we explored alternatives. We discovered the power of shared experiences, finding moments of connection through cuddling while watching our favorite shows, holding hands during evening walks, and even giving each other relaxing massages. It wasn't always textbook romance, but it was our way of expressing love and intimacy, unique and meaningful in its own way.

It wasn't always easy, let me tell you. There were moments of frustration, tears of exasperation, and days when the chaos felt overwhelming. But through it all, we held onto the love that brought us together. We communicated openly and honestly, expressing our needs and frustrations without judgment. We learned to laugh at the unexpected twists and turns our relationship threw our way, because sometimes, amidst the chaos, the humor was the only thing keeping us sane.

Most importantly, we never stopped believing in the power of our connection. We discovered that love, like a beautiful tapestry, is woven with threads of difference, acceptance, and unwavering support. It's not about creating a perfect picture, but about embracing the unique patterns and imperfections that make our love story truly special.

Creating External Structure and Routine

One of the key elements of building a strong connection with your partner is *creating external structure and routine.* Remember the "always-on" brain we discussed earlier? Sometimes, that constant internal stimulation can make it challenging to focus on tasks that require sustained attention, like spending quality time with you.

Here are some strategies to provide external structure:

1. **Vision board method:** Create a vision board together, depicting your shared goals, dreams, and aspirations. This visual reminder can help your partner stay focused and motivated, knowing they're working towards something bigger than the immediate task at hand.

2. **Scheduling "we time":** Block out dedicated time in your calendar for activities you both enjoy, whether it's a movie night, a walk in the park, or a romantic dinner. This ensures that quality time is prioritized and doesn't get lost in the daily shuffle.

3. **Implementing routines:** Establishing routines for common activities, like household chores or preparing for work, can provide a sense of predictability and structure. This can be particularly helpful for your partner, as it eliminates the need to make decisions on the fly and allows them to focus on completing the task at hand.

Building Shared Understanding Brick by Brick

Building a strong connection with your partner also requires shared understanding. Take time to learn about ADHD, its symptoms, and how it impacts their daily life. This doesn't require turning into an ADHD expert, but a basic understanding can go a long way in fostering empathy and compassion.

Here are some ways to build shared understanding:

i.   **Open communication:** Talk openly and honestly with your partner about their experiences and challenges related to ADHD. Ask questions, listen attentively, and avoid placing blame or judgment.

ii. **Read books and articles together:** Explore resources about ADHD together. This can spark meaningful conversations and help you both gain a deeper understanding of the condition.

iii. **Seek professional guidance:** If needed, consider seeking professional advice from a therapist or counselor who specializes in ADHD and couples' therapy. They can provide customized strategies for communication, conflict resolution, and fostering a healthy and fulfilling relationship.

Celebrating Progress and Igniting Passion

Let's be honest, focusing on the challenges of ADHD can be easy. But fostering a strong connection also involves celebrating progress, both big and small. Acknowledge and appreciate your partner's efforts, even if they seem insignificant. This positive reinforcement will encourage them to continue their efforts and foster a sense of accomplishment.

Don't forget to **ignite the passion** that brought you together in the first place. Plan special date nights, engage in activities you both enjoy, and keep the spark alive. Remember, connection thrives in the fertile soil of shared hobbies, meaningful conversations, and spontaneous adventures.

ADHD-Friendly Ways to Boost Intimacy

Let's address the elephant in the room: **intimacy** can sometimes feel challenging in a relationship with ADHD. The constant stimulation, difficulty focusing, and emotional dysregulation can all contribute to decreased intimacy or communication breakdowns.

But worry not, love warriors! Here are some *ADHD-friendly ways to boost intimacy:*

i. **Physical touch alternatives:** Not everyone feels comfortable with traditional forms of physical

Couples' Tool-Kit for Coping with ADHD| 69

intimacy. Explore alternative ways to connect physically, like cuddling on the couch while watching a movie, holding hands while walking in nature, or giving each other a relaxing massage.

ii. **Focus on quality over quantity:** Shorter, more frequent moments of connection can be more effective than trying to force a lengthy, uninterrupted session, which might prove challenging for your partner's focus and attention span.

iii. **Open communication:** Talk openly and honestly about your needs and desires regarding intimacy. Don't be afraid to experiment and find ways that work best for both of you.

The Power of Patience and Persistence

Building a strong connection with someone with ADHD takes patience, persistence, and a whole lot ...of love (cliché, but oh so true!). There will be days when the chaos feels overwhelming, and frustration threatens to simmer over. Remember, communication is key. Talk to your partner openly and honestly about your feelings, without placing blame or judgment. Listen actively to their perspective and work together to find solutions that address your individual needs.

Scheduling Weekly "State of the Union" Meetings

Communication doesn't have to be confined to moments of frustration. Establishing a regular routine of "State of the Union" meetings can be a powerful tool for fostering connection and understanding. Imagine this: once a week, carve out dedicated time, maybe over a cozy breakfast or a relaxing cup of tea, to simply talk. Not about the bills or the grocery list, but about your relationship, your feelings, and your needs.

Here are some tips for conducting effective "State of the Union" meetings:

i. **Set ground rules:** Agree on ground rules for the conversation, such as active listening, respectful communication, and avoiding blame.

ii. **Take turns sharing:** Set a timer and alternate taking turns sharing your feelings, frustrations, and positive experiences related to the relationship.

iii. **Focus on solutions:** Don't just dwell on problems, try to brainstorm solutions together. Be open to different perspectives and be willing to compromise.

iv. **End on a positive note:** Conclude your meeting by acknowledging each other's efforts and expressing appreciation for one another.

These "State of the Union" meetings can become a safe space for open communication, strengthening your connection and fostering a sense of teamwork in navigating the challenges of your relationship.

Remember, building a strong connection with someone with ADHD is a journey, not a destination. There will be bumps along the road, moments of frustration, and days when the chaos feels like it's winning. But amidst the whirlwind, there's also the potential for profound love, deep connection, and a shared story that's uniquely beautiful.

ACTION PLAN FOR CHAPTER 4

Activity 1: External Structure and Routine

Task:

- Create a visual daily schedule or checklist for both partners.

- Incorporate external cues like alarms or reminders for important tasks.

Benefits:

- Provides predictability and reduces overwhelm.

- Helps both partners stay organized and on track.

Real-Life Example:

Imagine creating a colorful daily schedule together, highlighting key activities such as work, meals, exercise, and relaxation time. Use sticky notes or a whiteboard to easily adjust the schedule as needed. When it's time for a meal or a break, set a timer or phone reminder to help with transitions.

Activity 2: Brick by Brick Understanding

Task:

- Schedule regular "Empathy Sessions" to discuss each other's perspectives and challenges.
- Use active listening techniques and empathy-building exercises.

Benefits:

- Enhances communication and empathy.
- Builds a deeper understanding of each other's experiences.

Real-Life Example:

Set aside dedicated time each week for an "Empathy Session" where you take turns sharing your thoughts and feelings without judgment. Use active listening by repeating back what you've heard to ensure understanding. For instance, if one partner struggles with time management, the other can express understanding and offer support rather than frustration.

Activity 3: Progress Celebration Rituals

Task:

- Establish a weekly "Wins of the Week" ritual.
- Celebrate achievements, big or small, with a special dinner, activity, or treat.

Benefits:

- Boosts morale and motivation.
- Reinforces positive behaviors and accomplishments.

Real-Life Example:

Every Sunday evening, gather together and share your "Wins of the Week" over a meal or dessert. These wins can be as simple as completing a project, sticking to a routine, or managing stress effectively. Celebrate each other's successes with genuine praise and encouragement.

Activity 4: Intimacy Boosters

Task:

- Create a shared vision board for your relationship goals and desires.
- Explore non-traditional forms of intimacy that cater to ADHD challenges.

Benefits:

- Fosters intimacy and connection.
- Encourages open communication about desires and needs.

Real-Life Example:

Sit down together with magazines, photos, and markers to create a relationship vision board. Include images or words that represent your shared goals, dreams, and desires. This visual representation can serve as a reminder of what you're working towards together. Additionally, for physical touch alternatives, consider activities like cuddling while watching a movie, giving foot massages, or practicing gentle yoga together.

Congratulations on completing the action plan for Chapter 4! By engaging in these activities, you're taking proactive steps to strengthen your connection and navigate the chaos of ADHD together. Remember, small efforts can lead to significant improvements in intimacy and understanding.

CHAPTER FIVE

The Peaceful Path Through Ups and Downs

You might feel like you're drowning in a sea of to-do lists, forgotten appointments, and misplaced socks, like your relationship with your husband is a constant game of catch-up. Trust me, I've been there. The frustration, the feeling of being unheard, the fear that you'll never be on the same page — it can leave you feeling like you're dancing to a different rhythm altogether.

But here's the thing — it doesn't have to be this way. I know, I know, it sounds like a cliche, but hear me out. There is a way to create a peaceful path through the ups and downs, a way to build a connection that thrives amidst the beautiful chaos that can come with loving someone with ADHD. Now, I'm not going to sugarcoat it — it won't always be sunshine and rainbows. But with some effort, understanding, and a whole lot of love, you can find your happily ever after, even in the whirlwind.

Talking about identifying and preventing triggers. My husband, bless his heart, has a knack for misplacing things. Keys, wallets, even entire grocery lists! It used to drive me crazy, like a constant reminder that I was the "responsible" one and he was the "scatterbrained" one. But then we realized it wasn't carelessness, it was his brain working differently. He thrives on bursts of energy, sometimes forgetting mundane tasks in the rush of creativity. So, we got a designated key holder, started using a shared grocery list app, and set reminders on his phone. Did it solve all our problems? Of course not! But it helped us anticipate the triggers and prevent them from turning into full-blown arguments.

Okay, so even with the best intentions, emotions can still run high. When the frustration bubbled over, I used to lash out, which only made things worse. My husband, wise man that he is, would try to reason, which felt like drowning in logic when I desperately needed a life raft of empathy. That's when we discovered the power of **calming tools**. He found solace in deep breathing exercises, while I swear by coloring intricate mandalas. Now, when the tension rises, we take a step back, use our calming tools, and come back to the conversation when we're both collected. Sometimes, it means taking a five-minute break in separate rooms, other times it means grabbing hands and taking a deep breath together. It's about acknowledging our emotions, finding individual ways to manage them, and coming back to the table with open hearts and clear heads.

Let's be honest, disappointments and impasses are inevitable. Missed deadlines, forgotten promises, the feeling of being let down – they can leave you feeling hurt and resentful. But instead of shutting down and building walls, we learned the importance of "repair attempts." After an argument, we don't just sweep it under the rug. We take the time to apologize, even if we don't feel entirely at fault, and offer genuine solutions.

"I know I forgot to pick up my dry cleaning again, and I understand you're frustrated," my husband might say, his voice gentle, his eyes sincere. "I'm really working on setting reminders on my phone, but is there something else I can do to make it up to you?"

It's not about placing blame, but about taking ownership of our actions and finding ways to rebuild trust. It's not always easy, especially when the hurt feels fresh, but we learned that communication, even the uncomfortable kind, is the bridge back to connection.

Here's a tip that was a game-changer for us — **couples counseling tailored for neurodiverse couples**. It gave us a safe space to communicate openly, learn about each other's perspectives, and develop healthy coping mechanisms. We met other couples navigating similar challenges, and realized we weren't alone. We learned tools like active listening, where you truly focus on understanding your partner's perspective, not just waiting to speak your own truth. We learned the power of "I" statements, like "I feel frustrated when..." instead of accusatory language. It wasn't about changing each other, but about understanding and appreciating our differences, and learning to dance to the music of our unique love story.

And lastly, remember this: **your partner is your teammate, not your adversary.** During those stormy times, when everything feels like it's falling apart, remember the friendship you built. Remember the laughter, the shared dreams, the reason you fell in love in the first place.

My husband and I met volunteering at a local animal shelter. He was this whirlwind of energy, throwing himself into playing with the dogs with infectious enthusiasm. I, on the other hand, found solace in quietly brushing the cats, their gentle purrs a ...soothing balm to my soul. We were opposites, drawn together by a spark we couldn't quite define.

It wasn't all sunshine and rainbows. There were days when the ADHD manifested in ways that felt overwhelming. Missed birthdays, forgotten anniversaries, unfinished projects scattered around the house like fallen leaves. It felt like a constant battle to be heard, understood, and appreciated.

But amidst the chaos, there was always the undercurrent of friendship. We shared a deep love for music, spending hours exploring new artists and reliving old favorites, singing along at the top of our lungs even if we were off-key. We had movie nights filled with popcorn, laughter, and the occasional playful debate over the "best movie ever." On weekends, we'd escape the city, venturing out on hikes where my husband's boundless energy fueled our explorations, while I found peace in the quiet beauty of nature.

These shared experiences, these moments of connection, were the lifeblood of our relationship. They were the reminders that beneath the challenges of ADHD, there was a **solid foundation of love and respect**. They were the anchors that held us steady during the emotional storms.

Finding ways to nurture the friendship outside the challenges of ADHD became our secret weapon. We started a tradition of "date nights in," where we cooked a new recipe together, the kitchen usually resembling a joyful (and slightly messy) experiment. We played silly board games, erupting in laughter as my husband's competitive spirit hilariously clashed with my strategy-focused approach. Or, we'd simply enjoy each other's company with a cup of tea and a good book, sharing the comfortable silence that spoke volumes about our connection.

We also embraced the power of humor. My husband's infectious laughter had the ability to melt away any lingering tension. We learned to laugh at the absurdities of the situation, like the time he forgot his wallet while on a grocery run, leading to a hilarious scavenger hunt for spare change in the car. It wasn't always about finding the perfect solution, but about finding the humor in the moment and appreciating the beautiful messiness of our love story.

Identifying and Preventing Triggers

For us, determining triggers was huge but didn't come intuitively for quirky ADHD brains. I had to gently explain seemingly small comments or environment factors completely dysregulated my emotions until meltdowns hit. Once we tracked patterns of what revs us up and why, preventing chaos got easier.

For instance, I learned giving open-ended decisions to Rich like "what do you feel like doing tonight" flustered him while specifics created security. Offering two concrete options based on intel of his current focus eased planning. We also use "if/then" thinking for avoiding classic hot spots like holidays, or when I take on too much then resent his freedom.

What clues signal impending emotional chaos for you two? Hunger, exhaustion, work stress? What relieves these before eruption? Brainstorm your unique preventative tactics so you both feel more secure addressing issues from regulated places, not reactive land mines.

Calming Tools When Emotions Run High

When upset strikes despite preventative planning, or unexpected chaos ambushes us, tangible calming tools help re-center before continuing tough talks.

We keep sensory bins around the house with fidget gadgets, headphones, or squishy stress balls. Even scented candles changed the energy. Walking separately to breathe deep for fifteen minutes makes space for hormones to settle so logic resumes.

Setting a vibrating smart watch timer ensures we reconvene in agreed upon moments. Journaling privately untangles swirling thoughts fueling frustration as well - getting them out constructs clarity. These tactics allow us to healthily self-soothe, then reunite with empathy restored.

Identify what short but tangible breaks serve you best in hot moments when they inevitably still arrive and make those resets part of your rhythm. The few minutes investing upfront prevents destructive words and widening distance between you after blowups. Space lands you back on the same team!

Recovering From Disappointments and Impasses

Unmet expectations and assumptions invite incredible hurt for ADHD partnerships in particular. Habitual lateness, distraction or impulsive decisions leading to financial or familial chaos fueled tremendous resentment for me initially until I better understood their neurological roots. Then empathy and accountability increased.

While my partner's brain wiring explains certain behaviors, it doesn't excuse them entirely without ownership or effort modifying patterns within his control. We had to find balance acknowledging symptoms while still taking responsibility for how they impact others.

Creating external structure around known distractibility gaps like calendars, medication alarms and household management systems prevented letdowns stemming from forgetfulness. Having game plans for balancing impulsiveness through accountability friends made spendy dreaming have fewer damaging outcomes when put into action incorrectly.

Approaching disappointments gently as a collective puzzle to continually solve together rather than an excuse for withdrawal or shame builds bridges through the inevitable.

Making Repair Attempts After Arguments

Like any marriage, we occasionally have conflicts or days tension pulls us apart even if we know neurological factors influence reactions. Early on, we made the mistake of extended silent treatments or retreating inward for long periods after disagreements which bred more distance.

Now we've learned to make repair attempts much faster even if resolution remains unfinished. This starts with verbalizing care for one another despite frustrations, then scheduling reconvenes times after short breathers so issues simmer rather than detonate.

For us, listening to understand rather than reacting with defensive intensity has helped exponentially. Seeking compromise through validating both realities, then getting creative on how to prevent hurts from both sides makes resolution reality, not chasing mirages.

Holding one another accountable while giving grace around symptoms morphs partnerships. I know Richard deeply wishes to follow through so believing his best intentions helps me grant patience and guidance to match his wiring with support.

Seeking Counseling Tailored for Neurodiverse Couples

While strong relationships rely on healthy coping strategies and letting little hurts lapse quickly, even the strongest benefit from professional support when patterns start feeling stuck. For us, couples counseling gifted hugely helpful perspective shifts around understanding ADHD differences.

Having research-based education around executive functioning gaps plaguing attention, retention, emotion regulation, activation and memory formation answered so many hurtful "Why can't you just..." questions fueled by ignorance, not indifference. Breaking behavioral cycles lingers infinitely more doable when both partners speak languages helping them understand themselves and one another accurately.

Good therapists coach compassion while still inspiring accountability, self-care and boundary tools. Finding ones specializing in neurodiversity proves key as their frameworks understand these relationships' unique rhythms. Equipped with insider strategies and empathy, we gained renewed strength tackling obstacles together rather than polarized apart.

If you two feel like you're talking in circles, enlist a guide to get unstuck. Even only briefly, having professional support builds fresh foundations worth the investment! The right fit counselor makes thriving reality, not wishful dreams.

Fostering Friendship to Weather Emotional Hurricanes

My final piece of hard-won advice? Don't lose sight that at its core, choose nurturing friendship in one another. During exhausting spells when resentment or numbness blankets hope, rewind to fond memories kindling your love. Watch favorite funny shows together to release tension. Reminisce sweet moments only you two share through inside jokes and treasured rituals. Play games inviting laughter and bonding once more.

Prioritizing emotional connection heals hurting. Savoring strengths shines light eclipsing flaws. When you remember your teammate awaits on the other side of struggles, motivation fuels persevering with compassion and communicating gently.

While ADHD hardly makes relationships easy, our once crumbling castle now stands stronger having weathered storms side by side. With pillow forts and dance parties punctuating pressures, we continue writing our story - one chapter closer because of every triumph and trial navigating this neurology altogether.

Rather than resenting differences, embrace support easing friction. As Rich and I learned, extending grace while seeking wisdom cultivates the kind of connection only forged through fire. We now help others thrive because we first had the courage to learn ourselves.

So, take heart - there is hope ahead wrought from the ashes of yesterday's exhaustion and hurt if you both dare take the hand beside you again. Healing awaits. You've got this!

ACTION PLAN FOR CHAPTER 5

Activity 1: Triggers Identification Exercise

Task:

- Sit down together and create a list of potential triggers for emotional dysregulation.
- Reflect on past incidents and identify patterns or common triggers.

Benefits:

- Increases awareness of potential triggers.
- Facilitates proactive steps to prevent emotional escalations.

Real-Life Example:

Imagine sitting down with your partner and creating a "Trigger Map." Draw a circle in the center of a piece of paper and label it "Emotional Dysregulation." Then, draw branches outwards, each representing a trigger such as lack of sleep, stress at work, or financial concerns. Discuss each trigger and its impact on emotions. By visualizing these triggers, you can develop strategies to avoid or manage them proactively.

Activity 2: Calming Toolbox Creation

Task:

- Compile a list of calming techniques that work for each partner.
- Create a physical or digital "Calming Toolbox" with these techniques.

Benefits:

- Provides immediate coping strategies during emotional highs.
- Encourages self-soothing and emotional regulation.

Real-Life Example:

Work together to brainstorm a list of calming techniques such as deep breathing exercises, meditation apps, listening to soothing music, or going for a walk. Create a physical toolbox with items like stress balls, essential oils, or a cozy blanket. When emotions run high, reach for the toolbox and choose a calming technique that feels right in that moment.

Activity 3: Recovery Rituals

Task:

- Establish a ritual for processing disappointments or impasses.
- Create a safe space for open and honest communication after challenging moments.

Benefits:

- Promotes healing and understanding after conflicts.
- Strengthens emotional bonds and resilience.

Real-Life Example:

Designate a cozy corner in your home as the "Recovery Zone." When either of you feels upset or overwhelmed, retreat to this space together. Start with deep breaths and then take turns expressing your feelings without interruption. Use "I" statements to communicate how you feel and what you need. Finish by sharing a comforting activity like watching a funny video or enjoying a favorite treat together.

Activity 4: Repair Attempt Protocol

Task:

- Develop a protocol for making repair attempts after arguments.
- Outline steps such as acknowledging impact, taking responsibility, and offering reassurance.

Benefits:

- Facilitates quicker resolution and forgiveness after conflicts.
- Builds trust and emotional safety within the relationship.

Real-Life Example:

Create a "Repair Attempt Checklist" together. This can include steps like:

i. Acknowledge impact: "I realize my words hurt you."

ii. Take responsibility: "I apologize for my part in the argument."

iii. Offer reassurance: "I value our relationship and want to work through this together."

Agree to use this checklist after arguments as a way to initiate healing and reconnecting.

Activity 5: Counseling Exploration

Task:

- Research and seek out counseling services tailored for neurodiverse couples.

- Schedule an initial consultation to explore options and discuss your needs.

Benefits:

- Provides professional guidance and support specific to your relationship.

- Offers a safe and neutral space to work through challenges.

Real-Life Example:

Research counseling services in your area that specialize in neurodiverse relationships. Look for therapists who have experience with ADHD and understand its impact on relationships. Schedule an initial consultation to discuss your goals and challenges. This step can be a proactive way to gain tools and insights from a professional.

Activity 6: Friendship Cultivation

Task:

- Plan regular "Friendship Dates" to strengthen your bond outside of daily responsibilities.
- Engage in activities that bring joy and laughter into your relationship.

Benefits:

- Nurtures friendship and camaraderie, essential for weathering storms.
- Provides a positive and fun outlet for both partners.

Real-Life Example:

Schedule a weekly "Friendship Date Night" where the focus is on enjoying each other's company. This could be trying a new restaurant, going for a hike, attending a comedy show, or simply playing board games at home. The key is to prioritize fun and connection, allowing you to build shared memories and strengthen your friendship.

Congratulations on completing the action plan for Chapter 5! By engaging in these activities, you're taking proactive steps to navigate the ups and downs of ADHD in your relationship. Remember, it's normal to face challenges, but with understanding, communication, and support, you can overcome them together.

CHAPTER SIX

Teamwork Makes the ADHD Dream

Work

Remember that hilarious scene in "The Incredibles" where Mr. Incredible tries to do everything himself, leading to utter disaster? Yeah, that's what a neurodiverse partnership can feel like sometimes, with one partner trying to shoulder all the responsibilities while the other, well, let's just say their focus might be elsewhere.

But hold on tight, love warriors, because with a little strategic planning and communication, we can turn this superhero movie into a romantic comedy! The key lies in aligning shared priorities and responsibilities.

Now, this isn't about playing the blame game or creating a rigid chore chart that resembles the Dewey Decimal System. It's about open and honest conversation. Talk about your individual strengths, weaknesses, and preferences. My husband, bless his heart, would happily spend hours meticulously organizing the spice rack (color-coded, no less!), while I'd rather tackle the mountain of laundry in record time.

So, we divided the responsibilities accordingly, playing to each other's strengths. He keeps the pantry organized, and I handle the laundry. It's not always 50/50, but it's a fair and balanced system that works for us.

But teamwork isn't just about chores. It's also about managing distractibility, which can be a real challenge for our partners with ADHD. Remember that time we spent hours planning our dream vacation to Italy, only to find my husband lost in the rabbit hole of "most scenic Italian coastal towns" on his phone? (Spoiler alert: we never made it to Italy that year.)

To combat this, we started implementing accountability checks. For important tasks, we set reminders, check in with each other regularly, and celebrate small wins along the way. It's not about micromanaging, but about providing gentle support and structure to help our partners stay focused and achieve their goals.

Speaking of goals, let's not forget the emotional and mental labor involved in a relationship. It's crucial to audit this division of labor too. Maybe your partner excels at planning social gatherings, while you find emotional support and listening easier. Recognizing each other's contributions in both practical and emotional spheres fosters a sense of teamwork and appreciation.

Now, here's a word to the wise: *patience is key.* Building a smooth-running team takes time and effort. There will be bumps in the road, moments of frustration, and days when you might want to throw in the towel (metaphorically, of course, because cleaning throws towels into the laundry basket, not at your partner).

Aligning on Shared Priorities & Responsibilities

Our first breakthrough happened finally accepting we organized life differently based on wiring, not worth or work ethic. I prized planning everything meticulously while my husband, rode passions' waves in the moment. Neither approach remained inherently "right" —just reflected core needs.

Once we embraced strengths didn't automatically indicate weaknesses elsewhere for either partner, playing into those talents eased resentment tremendously. We discovered discussing goals openly without assuming universal definitions of success prevented arguing over conflicting activities cramming calendars. Finding shared purpose transformed household tensions.

For instance, I manage most day-to-day finances and schedules while still consulting him, around vision setting and goals as leadership calms his distraction. We also share roles like cooking based on preference, not supposed gender norms. Overflowing harmony lived aligning responsibilities to attributes and communicating respectfully.

What innate strengths empower each of you? Get creative collaborating so both feel ownership based on skill sets, not overwhelming the stretched by dumping disabilities' deficits unfairly upon them. Shared visions and values prevent unspoken score-keeping tallying unseen sacrifices.

Traps to Avoid Around Household Tasks

Early on, we often pressured each other subtly reacting to differences rather than accepting supportively. Comments like "just set phone alerts" increased shame around ADHD symptoms already equated personal failure for him. I also wrongly assumed household chaos reflected disregard for me not executive function overload.

Gradually we realized words held power rousing emotions for good or ill. Blaming phrases often unintentionally belittled: "How could you forget? I told you!" Whereas compassion responses increased connection: "I know you want to follow through consistently too and your brain fights you. What support structures help this stick?"

Now chore balancing remains more collaborative than coerced. We adopted the "zone defense" concept where my partner manages upstairs tasks while I handle downstairs priorities without micromanaging across zones. If larger projects require all-hands efforts, we check-in successfully as a tag team. Assuming positive intent goes a long way!

Which phrases or perspectives empower progress when coordinating responsibilities? What landmines unintentionally shame? Getting on the same team prevents festering resentment.

Managing Distractibility to Do What Matters Most

One necessity I had to balance early when my partner, constantly got sidetracked was discerning his ADHD differences from dismissiveness towards me. Time after time, he'd lose track of conversations or commitments despite completely caring because executive functions falter splitting attention - not from indifference.

We learned the phrase "finishing well" to indicate when a topic required his total focus so tangents wouldn't unintentionally hijack priorities. Using activity boxes for containing distractions also minimized scatteredness during critical moments like paying bills.

Most importantly, discussing openly which tasks truly needed consistency, like medication or special dates versus flexible household items prevented micromanaging every misstep when only certain domains had harmful impacts if dropped. Realigning emphasis to strengths eased loads for us both.

Which routines or responsibilities feel non-negotiable to simplify? What requires patience and teamwork? Building in external supports like reminders or notebooks reduces distraction damage so you both breathe easier.

Accountability Checks for Mission Critical Tasks

For major priorities needing diligence, we initiated accountability check-ins. Initially, I'd pepper my partner with 20 questions every evening which overwhelmed him. Instead, we shifted to categorizing tasks as self-managed items versus weekly progress conversations around health, finances and family coordination requiring planning.

Setting reminders for revisiting bigger picture items monthly ensured we caught oversights early before small problems compounded majorly without micromanaging every detail. Coordinating peer support groups and coaches prevented insularity and kept growth ongoing behind scenes.

Most importantly, we framed accountability as opportunity celebrating wins, not examinations issuing sentences. Even imperfect progress deserves acknowledgement, not amplified angst. Share the load together - isolation breeds disaster.

What routine or responsibilities need collaboration? How could building in mutually agreed touchpoints foster success while preventing tunnel vision? Draft a checklist template to revisit finding healthy balance as life changes unfold.

Audit Your Division of Emotional & Mental Labor

An ongoing revelation as empty nesters was realizing mental checklists constantly consumed my mind preventing present moment connection unlike him simply riding life's waves with eager flexibility.

Invisible emotional and mental labor like remembering relatives' birthdays, scheduling doctor appointments, researching family vacation options and tracking dozens of ongoing household projects/finances drained joy and bondedness by rarely getting checked off fully.

Finally, we sat down dividing that managerial/emotional workload based on skill sets. My husband, spearheaded family fun planning and adventures booking while I coordinated caregiving logistics and volunteering priorities dear to me. Explicitly balancing efforts prevented assumed responsibilities snowballing silently over time - breeding bitterness when unaddressed.

What behind-the-scenes planning consumes either partner disproportionately right now? Make time quantifying then dividing those unseen tasks intentionally based on interest and time. Protect partnership from overload by valuing all contributions.

Coaching Each Other Through Situational Blind Spots

One keys nuance as a couple containing ADHD differences is acknowledging behavioral patterns requiring compassionate yet candid feedback for avoiding cumulative hurt when unchecked. This proves delicate territory not all readily welcome during defensiveness.

But entering gently emphasizing the "team" mentality means sharing constructive input protects the partnership above all. We often spot potential emotional collisions faster externally than when inside our own minds. Simply asking, "Would you like help navigating a situation I see tricky waters ahead?" build bridges safer than silence.

Especially during large gatherings like extended family trips where many moving pieces interplay, we agreed code phrases cuing discreetly when impulsive reactions require regulation in sensitive settings. Having pre-agreed cues deescalates without confrontation when emotions escalate.

What unique situational struggles could use gentle guardrails? Would code words help warn gently when approaching landmines? Get creative collaborating on positive signals respecting needs.

Be Patient: It Takes Years to Smooth Out the Wrinkles

If you're wondering whether weathering lifelong storms proves worth it, let our wrinkled smiles convince you - the messiness bonds beauty. No relationship blooms seamlessly without patience and teamwork.

What once overflowed resentment now overflows laughter as we parented little tornados together. Mornings kicking off amidst school chaos encapsulated our family perfectly. I'd be scheduling pediatrician appointments while my partner, danced silly jigs making pancakes to lift everyone's mood. We all bring different gifts benefitting the whole.

While ADHD never disappears, with understanding and emotional intelligence, its richness outshines limitations. Suddenly different journeys weave perfectly in rhythm together. But grace and grit build connections that endure.

ACTION PLAN FOR CHAPTER 6

Activity 1: Priority Alignment Exercise
Task:

- Sit down together and create a list of your individual priorities.
- Discuss and identify shared priorities as a couple.
- Merge the lists to create a combined set of shared priorities.

Benefits:

- Establishes clarity on shared goals and values.
- Facilitates better decision-making and task prioritization.

Real-Life Example:
Imagine sitting at the kitchen table with a stack of sticky notes and a marker. Each of you writes down your top three priorities on separate notes. These could be related to family, career, health, or personal growth. Then, come together and discuss similarities and differences. Combine the notes to create a joint set of shared priorities that you can refer to when making decisions or planning tasks.

Activity 2: Household Task Traps Avoidance

Task:

- Identify common traps that lead to task delays or overwhelm.

- Brainstorm solutions or strategies to avoid these traps.

Benefits:

- Improves efficiency and task management.

- Reduces frustration and feelings of being overwhelmed.

Real-Life Example:

Reflect on past instances where household tasks became overwhelming or were left incomplete. Perhaps a common trap is starting too many tasks at once or underestimating the time needed for certain chores. Create a "Task Traps Avoidance" list together, with solutions such as breaking tasks into smaller steps, setting timers, or using task management apps. Implement these strategies to make household tasks more manageable.

Activity 3: Distractibility Management Techniques

Task:

- Experiment with different techniques to manage distractibility.
- Identify what works best for each partner and incorporate into daily routines.

Benefits:

- Increases focus and productivity.
- Reduces frustration and stress related to distractibility.

Real-Life Example:

Try out techniques such as the Pomodoro Technique (working in focused intervals with short breaks), setting up a dedicated workspace with minimal distractions, or using noise-canceling headphones. Each partner can explore what works best for them and share their findings. For instance, if one partner finds that working in 30-minute focused intervals helps, they can communicate this to the other and create a supportive environment.

Activity 4: Accountability Checks Protocol
Task:

- Establish a regular check-in schedule for accountability.
- Define specific tasks and deadlines for accountability checks.

Benefits:

- Increases task follow-through and completion.
- Provides motivation and support for each other's goals.

Real-Life Example:
Set aside time each week for an "Accountability Check-In." Create a shared document or planner where you both list tasks and deadlines for the upcoming week. During the check-in, review progress, offer support, and celebrate achievements. For example, if one partner has a deadline for a work project, the other can offer to help with household tasks to free up time.

Activity 5: Emotional and Mental Labor Audit

Task:

- Reflect on the division of emotional and mental labor in your relationship.
- Discuss any imbalances and brainstorm solutions for a more equitable distribution.

Benefits:

- Promotes fairness and understanding.
- Reduces feelings of resentment or burnout.

Real-Life Example:

Take some time to individually journal about the emotional and mental tasks each of you typically handles. This could include managing schedules, remembering birthdays, or organizing family events. Compare notes and discuss any imbalances or areas where support is needed. Together, create a plan to redistribute tasks or offer more support in areas where one partner feels overwhelmed.

Activity 6: Blind Spot Coaching Sessions
Task:

- Schedule regular coaching sessions to support each other through blind spots.
- Practice active listening and offer constructive feedback.

Benefits:

- Enhances communication and understanding.
- Provides a safe space to address challenges and offer solutions.

Real-Life Example:
Designate a weekly "Coaching Session" where you take turns discussing challenges or blind spots you've noticed in each other. Use active listening skills to truly hear and understand each other's perspectives. Offer constructive feedback and brainstorm solutions together. For instance, if one partner struggles with time management, the other can offer gentle reminders or suggest time-blocking techniques.

Activity 7: Patience Cultivation

Task:

- Practice patience and understanding in everyday interactions.
- Create a mantra or reminder to stay patient during challenging moments.

Benefits:

- Fosters a supportive and understanding atmosphere.
- Reduces stress and conflict in the relationship.

Real-Life Example:

Choose a mantra together that reminds you to stay patient and understanding during moments of frustration. It could be something like, "We're in this together" or "Patience and kindness." Whenever you feel tensions rising, take a deep breath and repeat the mantra to yourself. This simple practice can shift the energy and help you approach challenges with a calm and patient mindset.

=

Congratulations on completing the action plan for Chapter 6! By engaging in these activities, you're taking proactive steps to strengthen teamwork and efficiency in your relationship. Remember, teamwork truly makes the ADHD dream work, and with patience and understanding, you can navigate the challenges together.

CHAPTER SEVEN

Parenting Playbook for ADHD Families

You might be feeling overwhelmed, like you're juggling a million balls – work, life, kids, and on top of it all, navigating the unique world of parenting with an ADHD partner. Trust me, I've been there. The extra dose of chaos, the feeling of being the "responsible" one, the worry about your kids – it can feel like you're constantly walking a tightrope.

But here's the thing – you don't have to do this alone. Just like we learned to build a fulfilling relationship with our ADHD partner, we can create a **thriving family environment,** one where everyone feels supported, understood, and loved for who they are. It won't always be easy, but with some communication, creativity, and a whole lot of compassion, you can create a haven where both your children and your partner can flourish.

Let's talk about **supporting your partner**. My husband is an amazing father, full of boundless energy and infectious enthusiasm. But his ADHD can manifest in ways that impact his parenting style. He might struggle with routines, forget important appointments, or get easily sidetracked during playtime. The key here is *understanding* and *collaboration*. Instead of criticizing or nagging, I try to be his cheerleader. If getting out the door in the morning feels like a marathon, I'll jump in and help with the packing or offer calming suggestions.

We also learned the power of **co-parenting strategies**. My husband thrives on visual cues, so we created a chore chart with pictures and stickers. I take the lead on bedtime routines, which require more structured consistency, while he excels at engaging our children in imaginative play sessions. It's about playing to each other's strengths and creating a system that works for the whole family.

Now, let's talk about the most important people in the room – *your children*. Having a parent with ADHD can be confusing for them at times. They might see the struggles, the forgetfulness, the bursts of energy that sometimes lead to frustration. But here's the secret weapon: encouragement.

Focus on your partner's positive qualities. My husband makes the goofiest jokes, tells the most mesmerizing bedtime stories, and has a knack for turning everyday errands into mini-adventures. When our kids see how much joy and love he brings into their lives, they learn to accept and appreciate his differences.

Instilling confidence and self-acceptance is crucial, both for your children and your partner. Talk openly about ADHD, not in a negative light, but as a unique way of thinking and processing the world. Encourage your children to understand and embrace their own strengths and challenges, just like they're learning to embrace their father's.

Building a family with an ADHD partner is a journey, not a destination. There will be moments of frustration, days when you question everything, and times when the chaos feels overwhelming.

As the squealing laughter of our mini-mes chases our dog out back, I can't believe the wild ride since becoming parents over a decade ago! When hubby and I first met, my freewheeling spontaneity enchanted his grounded loyal heart. But after "I dos," reality hit hard juggling chaos with his ADHD and my spirited temperament. Many moments tested whether this partnership could withstand the pressures of parenting amidst already swirling differences. Yet here we are, white-haired and wiser, watching our babies flourish into kindhearted leaders.

As I watch my partner pretending to soar like a superhero with our giggling toddler, I can't help but smile thinking back on the unexpected parenting adventure we've navigated over the last few years. When we first started dating, his spontaneous spirit balanced my tendency to plan everything down to a T. But soon impulsiveness and distractibility that once intrigued me brought chaos, especially after a surprise pregnancy turned life upside down.

Suddenly, overflowing days of feedings, tantrums, and messes met head-on with ADHD challenges focusing amid constant distractions. My anxiety brain spiraled with worries amplified by sleeplessness. Finding aligned approaches felt impossible between opposite wiring.

Yet somehow, embracing empathy, playfulness and teamwork eases friction. Parenting a neurodiverse child alongside an ADHD co-pilot brings beautifully messy rewards if you dare lean in! Here's what helped us laugh more and stress less so far:

Supporting Your Partner's Parenting Journey

As a perfectionist planner, I prided myself in managing schedules and details. But I'd often micromanage my partner's approaches when they appeared too relaxed or whimsical, failing to account for ADHD differences. "You forgot her doctor's appointment - how could you!" I'd criticize, assuming my way worked best.

The turning point was realizing our daughter needed nurture in complementary forms from each of us. I provided security through order. He offered connection via laughter and confidence boosting. Once embracing collaboration over critique, she blossomed exponentially.

What innate strengths fill your parenting gaps? Get creative so both feel empowered based on abilities, not overwhelmed unfairly by weaknesses. Your differences can strengthen development beautifully!

Co-Parenting Strategies Across ADHD Differences

My detail-driven nature handled endless organizing easily. But his executive function gaps wrestled even basic sequential tasks, testing my need for control. Preventing resentment meant accepting realistic responsibilities aligned to our respective attributes and limitations anxiety and ADHD posed.

He now tackles hands-on priorities like checking homework and meal prep, easing overwhelm, while I spearhead coordinating routines suiting my detail-orientation. We all contribute unique gifts benefitting this family mosaic when responsibility divides fairly by capabilities. And quick daily alignment check-ins keep us paddling in sync!

What roles best fit each parent's innate capabilities? Where might you both give grace while seeking collaborative solutions? Find empowerment together!

Helping ADHD Kids Thrive with Encouragement

In families like ours, there's a 50% chance our child might demonstrate attention or emotional regulation differences too. As she's grown, my partner's insider empathy guiding her ADHD wiring through creative confidence building has proven invaluable. He nurtures her exuberance as strength rather than weakness.

Meanwhile, my stability offers grounded reassurance amidst any chaos as we gently coach coping skills preventing shutdowns. I had to release rigid expectations about performance reflecting self-worth to make space for her unique flowering, not force fitting to norms.

What support could help your child's needs feel embraced, not pressured to fit constraining molds? Get creative together championing their inner light!

Instilling Confidence & Self-Acceptance

My deepest longing has been nurturing self-acceptance prospering through challenges differently, like her father. His ADHD bred lifetime "too muchness" messages masking incredible talents. Vulnerably sharing his experiences builds connection and compassion, coaching that she can harness uniqueness as superpower too. Soon, chaos finds empowered calibration.

What messages might your child absorb about self-worth from responses to their needs? How could you nurture self-love instead through unconditional support?

How To Kindly Educate Family Members About ADHD

Well-meaning relatives often overload us with narrow perspectives about "correcting" behaviors without realizing neurodiversity drives differences. My parents frequently express concerns her spirited nature demonstrates defiance or damage somehow.

But explaining ADHD compassionately as wiring, not character flaw opened their eyes towards acceptance and accommodation. "Her brain processes the world uniquely needing more patience but she has such a sweet heart!" Suddenly, problem-solving replaced cold shoulders as we identified supportive solutions together.

What loved ones might benefit from kind insights around ADHD's impact? Plant seeds opening their eyes with patient grace! Protect your peace and child's confidence.

While the messiness continues some days barely keeping heads above water parenting amid neurodiversity, the beauty blooming through bonding together outweighs hardship. We're still figuring out graceful rhythms but meeting each challenge with resilience, playfulness and compassion continues unfolding incredible joy on this adventure built for two, now blossomed into three!

ACTION PLAN FOR CHAPTER 7

Activity 1: Supporting Your Partner in Parenting

Task:

- Take turns sharing your feelings and experiences about parenting a child with ADHD.
- Practice active listening and offer empathy and support to your partner.

Benefits:

- Strengthens your bond as a couple.
- Enhances understanding and teamwork in parenting.

Real-Life Example:

Set aside a quiet evening to have a "Parenting Check-In" session. Each of you takes turns sharing your challenges, victories, and emotions related to parenting your child with ADHD. Practice active listening without interruption, and then offer words of encouragement and understanding. For example, if your partner expresses frustration about managing homework time, you can offer to take on some tasks to lighten their load.

Activity 2: Co-Parenting Strategies Across Differences

Task:

- Identify each other's strengths and how they can complement each other in parenting.

- Create a visual representation (such as a Venn diagram) of overlapping strengths for unified parenting.

Benefits:

- Promotes a unified approach to parenting.

- Utilizes each other's strengths for effective co-parenting.

Real-Life Example:

Sit down together with a whiteboard or paper. Draw two intersecting circles representing each of your strengths as parents. In the overlapping area, write down strategies or tasks where you can collaborate effectively. For instance, if one of you is great at creating routines while the other excels in creative problem-solving, you might find a perfect overlap in creating a fun and structured homework routine.

Activity 3: Encouraging ADHD Kids to Thrive

Task:

- Create a "Success Jar" for your child, where you both write down and celebrate their achievements.
- Implement a reward system with tangible incentives for completing tasks or exhibiting positive behavior.

Benefits:

- Boosts your child's self-esteem and motivation.
- Provides positive reinforcement for desired behaviors.

Real-Life Example:

Get a jar and colorful slips of paper. Each time your child accomplishes something, whether it's completing homework without reminders or showing kindness to a sibling, write it down on a slip and put it in the jar. At the end of the week, gather as a family to read the slips and celebrate together. Additionally, create a reward system where your child earns points for completing tasks or showing positive behavior, which can be exchanged for privileges or small treats.

Activity 4: Instilling Confidence and Self-Acceptance

Task:

- Engage in "Strength Spotting" with your child, where you highlight their unique talents and qualities.
- Have regular conversations about self-acceptance and resilience.

Benefits:

- Nurtures a positive self-image in your child.
- Equips your child with tools to handle challenges.

Real-Life Example:

Make it a habit to point out your child's strengths and positive attributes daily. For example, during dinner, each family member can share one thing they admire or appreciate about the child. This fosters a supportive environment where your child feels valued. Additionally, have open discussions about accepting oneself, including both strengths and areas for growth. Share stories of your own challenges and how you overcame them to inspire your child.

Activity 5: Educating Family Members on ADHD

Task:

- Host a family meeting or virtual session to educate relatives about ADHD.
- Prepare a presentation with basic information, common misconceptions, and how they can support your child.

Benefits:

- Builds a network of understanding and support for your child.
- Reduces stigma and increases empathy from family members.

Real-Life Example:

Invite family members to an "ADHD Awareness Night" where you provide an informative presentation. Include facts about ADHD, common challenges your child faces, and strategies that work well for them. Share personal anecdotes and experiences to make it relatable. Encourage family members to ask questions and offer suggestions for how they can support your child. This not only educates but also strengthens your family's support system.

Congratulations on completing the action plan for Chapter 7! By engaging in these activities, you're taking proactive steps to support your partner, foster your child's growth, and educate your family about ADHD. Remember, you are a team, and together you can create a nurturing and understanding environment for your child to thrive.

CHAPTER EIGHT

Thriving Together Through the Years

Let's talk about the **long haul.** You've navigated the initial bumps, learned to communicate effectively, and built a foundation of understanding with your ADHD partner. But now, you might be wondering, "What about the future? Can this love actually last?"

Let me tell you, it absolutely can, and not just last, but **thrive.** It takes effort, sure, but the journey of continuing to fall in love with each other's unique selves is an incredibly rewarding one.

Remember, your partner, with their ADHD quirks, is the same person you fell head over heels for. Their infectious enthusiasm, their creative spark – these are still there, waiting to be rediscovered and appreciated. It's about celebrating their strengths and understanding that their differences are not shortcomings, but rather unique pieces that make up the beautiful puzzle of your relationship.

Talking about the love language of an ADHD partner. It might not always be roses and sonnets, but it's there, expressed in their own way. My husband, bless his heart, isn't the most verbally expressive person, but his way of showing love is through his actions. He remembers the little things, like my favorite brand of coffee or the way I like my eggs cooked in the morning. His spontaneous bursts of energy sometimes translate into unexpected adventures, like a last-minute road trip or a surprise picnic in the park. Learning to appreciate these unique expressions of love can deepen your connection and strengthen the bond you share.

Speaking of connection, let's address the elephant in the room: intimacy with ADHD. It can be challenging, but it's definitely not impossible. Open communication is key. Talk about your needs and desires, be patient and understanding, and explore different ways to connect. Remember, intimacy goes beyond the physical. Shared experiences, emotional connection, and simply enjoying each other's company are all crucial aspects of a fulfilling relationship.

Now, here's a word on **independence and interdependence:** You are two individuals, each with your own needs and desires. It's important to **nurture your independence,** pursue your hobbies, and spend time with friends. This doesn't diminish the importance of **interdependence** within the relationship. Support each other's dreams, celebrate each other's successes, and be there for each other through challenges. It's a beautiful dance of respecting each other's space while also building a life together.

Speaking of building a life together, **keeping the passion alive** is essential. Don't get stuck in a rut! Plan **shared activities and adventures**, even if they're small. Take a cooking class together, explore a new neighborhood, or go on a weekend getaway. These shared experiences create lasting memories and remind you why you fell in love in the first place.

As my partner unexpectedly dips and kisses me beneath twinkling reception lights, I'm overwhelmed by gratitude for the story unfolding since first crossing paths at a friend's wedding years ago. Neither of us expected my tendency towards overanalyzing situations and perfectionist planning would mesh well with his spontaneous ADHD heart wired to ride passions' waves. Yet here we sway tenderly having weathered every storm and milestone side-by-side with resilience, empathy and choice recovering intimacy each time life pulled us apart.

Early on, I falsely assumed marriage would eradicate differences and struggles. But as stress compounded, polarities exacerbated disconnect rather than unity prevailing if unchecked. I'd criticize his distractibility sabotaging responsibilities. He'd withdraw from the intensity, fueling shame and desperation in me.

The turnaround emerged finally accepting we're organized differently based on neurology, not indifference towards each other. I prized planning. He thrived on passion's spontaneity. Once embracing strengths lacking elsewhere didn't reflect love's absence but rather opportunities for nurturing teamwork, yin met yang beautifully. He spearheads adventure. I supply steadiness. When leverage points clicked collaborating interdependently, suddenly home felt harmonious.

What innate abilities empower each of you? Get creative sharing strengths so covering weaknesses prevents overburdening unfairly. Help write each other's story with grace.

Love & Sex for ADHD Couples

As opposites attracting explorers, no surprise neurodiversity played into romance's rhythms too! My tendency overanalyzing often paralyzed spontaneity while his distraction numbed attentiveness to emotional or physical intimacy needs brewing disconnect. We had to fight to reclaim playfulness amidst parenting stressors pile-driving libido and laughter to extinction.

Escaping for hotel staycations, dancing in the rain to favorite songs and trying couples athletic contests reawakened fiery chemistry hindered by everyday exhaustion and phones constantly competing for his cognition when I craved presence. Removing distractions to focus solely on affection and verbal reassurance reset security in feeling cherished. Soon bits of predicable chaos faded behind love's curtain call back to center stage spotlight where this romance once unfolded.

What unique needs do each of you have for securing passion's durability? Make sharing them weekly priority. Flirtation is the fountain of youth for lifelong love! Reconvene consistently.

Nurturing Independence Alongside Interdependence

Early on, I falsely assumed true soul mates must desire total physical closeness, shared hobbies and 100% joint decision-making. But attempting to force-fit this fantasy eroded my partner's emotional bandwidth needing more introverted processing time I initially perceived as rejection instead of understanding sensory overload risks present for him managing ADHD.

The turning point emerged agreeing loving each other well meant nurturing personal interests and friendships alongside coupledom, not forsaking all individual identities sacrificially. I joined a book club. He regularly met guy friends at concerts unwinding without guilt for needing stimulation I couldn't provide constantly.

Carving regular separation prevented resentment accumulating from unvoiced needs. Then coming back together intermittently revived fondness and attraction. Absence does make the heart grow fonder when balanced alongside togetherness! We could each give and receive better love having breather spaces supporting self-care.

What independent outlets might help refill your oxygen tanks regularly? Schedule that solace preemptively so busyness doesn't accidentally isolate. Protect partnership from depletion.

Renewing Passion Through Shared Activities & Adventure

Now deeply rooted as empty nesters climbing career ladders amidst midlife changes, we have to fight to block out couple time reconnecting mutually enjoyable activities that first spun our love story. But it remains so worthwhile not losing each other in daily hustle's noise! We began scheduling weekly "just us" dates trying new restaurants, then strolling beaches reminiscing sans distractions.

Weekend hiking getaways also helped when deeper life vision conversations required revisiting away from routine demands. Carving space for leisure, laughter and creative play reawakened the fun-loving friends beneath responsible adults toiling tirelessly. Setting phone boundaries and escaping from roles revived forgotten facets of identity only the other's safety saw. Partnership is the gift that keeps giving when nourished!

What might you two schedule, ensuring couple time blocked monthly? Dare a weekly date night mixing classics with new novelties? See what memories can be made together!

Visioning Meaning & Purpose for Years to Come

In this season with retirement around the corner as empty nesters, my partner and I are taking time reflecting on what calls us forward up the mountain ahead now the terrain shifts. While ADHD often orients his enthusiasm living spontaneously in each moment's beauty which differs from my leaning into preparedness, articulating motivations openly grounds our vision in possibility.

I know his wiring gifts gorgeous zeal for seizing today. My stability anchors navigating towards tomorrow. And having space to voice those values compassionately without judgment sets course for this next chapter's meaning made side-by-side. We're still exploring aligned legacy dreams but meeting each sunrise together seems the perfect place to start!

If what energizes tomorrow differs from your partner, make time unpacking it without assumptions. See each other's longings, let go limitations and collaborate on compromise unveiling richest life maps integrating every journeyer's voice. This is just another adventure beginning!

As my love encircles me closely renewing vows to finish this sweet dance, eyes brimming with tears of gratitude for weathering every past storm, I know choosing relentless empathy transformed pain into passion. Each fractured yesterday, through resilience, builds bridges towards healing heart by heart, hand in hand moving forward. So, take courage, my friend. Two dreams daring to believe brokenness can turn beautiful is where the wildest love stories wait unveiling. And yours has just begun!

ACTION PLAN FOR CHAPTER 8

Activity 1: Love Letters to Each Other's Strengths
Task:

- Write a love letter to your partner highlighting their unique strengths and qualities.
- Exchange these letters on a special date night or when you need a reminder of each other's positive traits.

Benefits:

- Deepens emotional connection and appreciation.
- Helps in refocusing on positive aspects during challenging times.

Real-Life Example:

Set aside time to reflect on your partner's strengths. Write a heartfelt letter expressing gratitude and admiration for these qualities. For instance, if your partner's creativity shines through in their problem-solving, express how their innovative approach has positively impacted your life. Exchange these letters on a date night, creating a beautiful reminder of your love and appreciation for each other.

Activity 2: Intimacy Building Exercises

Task:

- Practice mindfulness together with guided meditation or deep breathing exercises.
- Engage in non-sexual physical touch sessions to reconnect and reduce stress.

Benefits:

- Enhances emotional intimacy and reduces stress.
- Fosters a sense of closeness and connection.

Real-Life Example:

Choose a quiet evening to practice mindfulness together. Use a guided meditation app or YouTube video to lead you through a calming session. Focus on breathing and being present with each other. Additionally, set aside time for non-sexual physical touch sessions. This could be a gentle back massage, holding hands, or cuddling while watching a movie. These activities promote relaxation and strengthen the bond between partners.

Activity 3: Balancing Independence and Interdependence

Task:

- Schedule solo activities that each partner enjoys to promote independence.
- Plan joint activities where you can collaborate and share experiences.

Benefits:

- Encourages personal growth and self-expression.
- Strengthens the bond through shared experiences.

Real-Life Example:

Designate specific days or evenings for solo activities. This could be pursuing a hobby, going for a walk alone, or attending a class. Encourage your partner to explore their interests and passions independently. On other days, plan joint activities where you can collaborate, such as cooking a new recipe together, going for a hike, or attending a workshop. This balance allows for personal growth while nurturing your connection as a couple.

Activity 4: Adventure Date Nights

Task:

- Create a list of adventurous activities you both want to try.
- Schedule regular "Adventure Date Nights" to explore these activities together.

Benefits:

- Adds excitement and novelty to the relationship.
- Sparks new conversations and shared memories.

Real-Life Example:

Sit down together and brainstorm a list of adventurous activities you've always wanted to try. This could include rock climbing, attending a cooking class, or taking a spontaneous road trip. Schedule these as "Adventure Date Nights" on your calendar. Make it a fun challenge to check off activities from your list. These shared adventures create lasting memories and keep the relationship dynamic and exciting.

Activity 5: Creating a Vision Board Together

Task:

- Gather magazines, scissors, glue, and a board or paper.
- Create a vision board representing your shared dreams and goals for the future.

Benefits:

- Provides clarity and focus on shared aspirations.
- Strengthens commitment and motivation towards your vision.

Real-Life Example:

Set aside a creative evening to work on your vision board together. Cut out images and phrases from magazines that represent your collective dreams, whether it's traveling the world, starting a family project, or achieving career milestones. Arrange these on a board or paper, creating a visual representation of your shared vision. Display the vision board in a prominent place where you can both see it daily, reminding you of your goals and aspirations.

Congratulations on completing the action plan for Chapter 8! By engaging in these activities, you and your partner are taking proactive steps to nurture your relationship, deepen your connection, and envision a meaningful future together. Remember, love is an ongoing journey, and with effort and dedication, you can continue to thrive as a couple.

CONCLUSION

As I snuggle my sleeping son while writing these final words, overwhelming gratitude washes over me for the unexpected gifts this neurodiverse journey has uncovered. When Jack and I collided in marriage without comprehending ADHD's impacts years ago, perpetual chaos and hopeless resentment defined days. I scorned his distracted forgetfulness sabotaging security blanketing my world. He internally absorbed blow after blow as anxiety brewed beneath my external frustration frothing forth. Reactivity ruled the rhythms echoing more torment than haven.

Yet somehow in the messiness, glimmers of light shone through cracks formed under pressure eventually. In daring vulnerability before counseling clinicians urging us "try harder," breakthrough took root. naming the nameless beast plaguing passion and unity suddenly explained exhausting efforts amounting to lonely nil heretofore. Newly informed, we gained access to courage conquering symptoms once deemed terminal regarding relationships surviving.

Armed with science-backed education, medication modifications, emotional regulation coaching and most significantly – a paradigm shift from playing tug-of-war to unified encouragement – we transformed turmoil into tools planting seeds of support, resilience and joy once deemed impossible.

Healthy communication, boundary setting, treatment plan alignments to need and focusing first on friendship fertilized an ecosystem where neurodiversity could flourish beyond limitation. I learned embracing interdependency despite pride's pull. Jack unpacked masking behaviors obscuring windows for the world to know his incredible soul beyond symptoms. And in the journeying, we fell in love all over again.

If your home currently hides hurt and misunderstanding more than harmony, take heart, my friend...there is hope awaiting! With compassion as your compass guided by wisdom and grit's grace, soon you'll stand on mountaintops grinning too having weathered the storms. No relationship survives on smooth seas alone. But two hands joined together with informed empathy steering ships makes thriving through turbulence guaranteed. Your love story's next courageous chapter begins today!

Made in United States
Troutdale, OR
04/24/2024

19434617R00086